Sound Trackers

Reggae

SOUND TRACKERS – REGGAE
was produced by

David West Children's Books
5-11 Mortimer Street
London W1N 7RH

Picture research: Brooks Krikler Research
Editor: Clare Oliver
Consultant: Dan Brooks

First published in Great Britain in 1998 by
Heinemann Library, Halley Court, Jordan Hill, Oxford OX2 8EJ, a division of
Reed Educational and Professional Publishing Limited.

OXFORD MELBOURNE AUCKLAND KUALA LUMPUR
SINGAPORE IBADAN NAIROBI KAMPALA JOHANNESBURG
GABORONE PORTSMOUTH NH CHICAGO

01 00 99 98
10 9 8 7 6 5 4 3 2 1

ISBN 0 431 09104 8 (HB)
ISBN 0 431 09108 0 (PB)

British Library Cataloguing in Publication Data

Brunning, Bob
Reggae. - (Sound trackers)
1. Reggae music - Juvenile literature
I. Title
781. 6 ' 46

Printed and bound in Italy.

Reggae

Bob Brunning

Heinemann

CONTENTS

On these discs is a selection of the artists' recordings. Many of these albums are now available on CD. If they are not, many of the tracks from them can be found on compilation CDs.

Dennis Brown

These boxes give you extra information about the artists and their times.
Some contain anecdotes about the artists themselves or about the people who helped their careers or, occasionally, about those who exploited them.
Others provide historical facts about the music, lifestyles, fans and fashions of the day.

INTRODUCTION

It is astonishing that one tiny Caribbean island, Jamaica, should be the main source of a style of music which is known all over the world: reggae.

Of course, the history of reggae is complex. As with blues and jazz, reggae's roots can be found in Africa. It is generally considered that reggae itself has developed from mento, a traditional form of Jamaican folk music. Folk music has traditionally been a vehicle for protest songs, and mento was no exception,

A reggae band plays at Sunsplash, the annual Jamaican Song Festival.

railing against injustice, racism and corruption. But, as with the blues music which developed in the USA under similar circumstances, the strong message was made palatable by its powerful, danceable beat.

Reggae has a serious side which sets it apart from other popular music. It has close links with Rastafarianism, a religion based around the Bible but re-interpreted from a black perspective. Its followers consider Africa their spiritual home. Reggae songs also deal with more down to earth problems, such as unemployment, education, poverty… and affairs of the heart!

In defining reggae, 'Toots' Hibbert of the Maytals puts it: "Reggae means coming from the people. Everyday things, like from the ghetto. We put music to it, make a dance out of it. I would say that reggae means coming from the roots, ghetto music. Means poverty, suffering and in the end, maybe union with God if you do it right."

ASWAD

Aswad were one of the most important and influential UK reggae bands and popularised political black music. Even their name is political, taken from the Arabic for 'black'. Inspired by the success of Bob Marley, the band aimed to combine their Rastafarian beliefs with comment on social issues of the 1970s and '80s, such as racism and poverty.

BACK TO AFRICA

Formed in 1975 by Brinsley 'Dan' Forde and drummer Angus Gaye, the band also featured George Oban on bass and the Jamaican singer Donald Griffiths. Aswad soon found a voice of their own and approached the premier UK 'black' label, Island, with their demos. Executive Leslie Palmer was interested enough to take a chance with Aswad, and released their first single, 'Back to Africa' in '76. Although not a major hit, this debut sold enough to encourage Island to release another single in the same year. The band's first album, 'Aswad', followed a few months later.

LIFE IN THE GHETTO

Aswad were based in West London. Living in poor quality accommodation, the band experienced at first hand the realities of racial harassment and relative poverty. They were fiercely determined to express these experiences through their music.

'Aswad'
June '76
'Hulet'
April '78
'New Chapter of Dub'
September '82

'To The Top'
September '86
'Crucial Tracks: The Best Of Aswad'
April '89
'The Wicked'
October '90

MUSICAL DIFFERENCES

But before long, there was conflict within the band. Keyboard player Courtney Hemmings left and in came Tony 'Gad' Robinson. The friction cost the band some time.

6

In 1978, the band released the album 'Hulet', to the delight of their loyal followers. However, the band members were still at odds over the musical direction they wanted to take. Frustrated, founder members Oban and Griffiths left the band.

SOUND TRACKERS

But Aswad were about to enjoy an unexpected lift to their career. Brinsley Forde landed the lead in 'Babylon', Franco Rosso's film about reggae music which was released in 1980. The accompanying soundtrack album featured two of Aswad's most impressive singles: 'Rainbow Culture' and 'Warrior Charge'.

SUCCESS

After two albums for CBS, Aswad returned to Island for their first live album, recorded in 1982 at the Notting Hill Carnival, the UK's biggest black festival.

Two moderately successful singles followed: '54-46 That's My Number' (originally recorded by Toots Hibbert), and 'Chasing The Breeze'. In '86, Aswad recorded an acclaimed album, 'To The Top'. Not before time, they enjoyed their first No. 1 hit with 'Don't Turn Around' in '88. The band remains one of the UK's most exciting reggae outfits.

RASTA ROOTS

Rastafarianism is a religion born, like reggae, in the West Indies. Followers reinterpret the Bible in black terms. In 1916, the black activist Marcus Garvey had prophesied "Look to Africa for the crowning of a Black King; he shall be the Redeemer". When Prince Regent Ras Tafari became Emperor of Ethiopia in 1930, Rastafarians saw this as the fulfilment of Garvey's prophecy – this king was the new Messiah. The Emperor took the name Haile Selassie, meaning 'Might of the Trinity'.

According to Rasta belief, Haile Selassie I (right) was the living God.

Aswad is just one of many reggae bands to combine Rasta beliefs and social commentary in its music, in the hope of promoting racial tolerance.

DENNIS BROWN

People tend to assume that reggae artists come from deprived backgrounds. How else can they write genuine songs of protest, highlighting poverty and prejudice? Yet one of the finest and best-loved reggae singers, Dennis Emmanuel Brown, came from a respectable middle-class household. Born in 1957, son of a TV scriptwriter, Brown stayed at school until he was 17 years old – later than average for youngsters of the time.

CHILD STAR
However, as for many reggae artists, Brown's musical career started early. He was writing and singing at the age of eleven. By the time he was 13, Brown was signed to the prestigious Studio One record label based in Kingston, Jamaica, owned by Clement Coxsone Dodd.

MUSIC LESSONS
But Brown never felt that music got in the way of his education: "Working with Downbeat (Dodd's sound system) was like going to a college because you had all the people that was happening at the time there. They had people like Alton Ellis, the Heptones, Lascelles Perkins, Lloyd James and John Holt. Coxsone was the ace producer at the time."

Producer Clement Coxsone Dodd, owner of Studio One.

On the record label:

'No Man Is An Island'
June '70
'Super Reggae and Soul Hits'
July '72
'Wolf & Leopards'
October '78

THIS BOOK BELONGS TO
TRINITY SCHOOL
SHIRLEY PARK, CROYDON
TEL. 081-656 9541

'Money In My Pocket'
October '79
'Super Hits'
June '83
'The Prime of Dennis Brown'
October '93

NO BOY IS AN ISLAND

In 1969 Dennis Brown released his first single, a version of the Impressions' 'No Man Is An Island' – five years before he left school! It was a big local hit, as was its follow-up 'If I Follow My Heart'. The early '70s saw Brown flitting between record labels, and working with a succession of excellent producers. In '74 he met the talented producer Winston 'Niney' Holness. Together they made some of Dennis' finest recordings, including the albums 'Just Dennis' and 'Wolf & Leopards'.

MONEY IN HIS POCKET?

As early as 1974, Dennis had toured the UK with Toots and the Maytals, but he had to wait another five years before achieving international recognition – and even then some feel he never achieved the acclaim he richly deserved. Ten years into his career, 'Money In My Pocket' and 'Ain't That Loving You' gave Brown the breakthrough he had been waiting for. He signed a deal with the huge record label A&M and moved to London. At the same time, he became involved in the small Jamaican label DEB as a producer and writer.

ROOTS REGGAE

Not all of Brown's albums and singles were great commercial successes, but his heartfelt commitment to his Rasta roots, and his beautiful, soulful voice ensured the unfailing support of a large fan base. His concerts were always well attended and he never performed a bad show.

TODAY

Dennis Brown has been rather quiet in the late '80s and early '90s, but he has never ceased to write, perform and record his original and often moving material.

CULTURAL HARMONY

Like so many other reggae artists and fans, Dennis Brown is a devout Rastafarian and considers Africa his homeland: "Africa? Africa? Just the mention of it, man, is like you call my name. Africa is the motherland and Africa is where we rightly belong. And that's where I want to be."

But it was Brown's time in London that really opened his eyes to how different communities could live together in harmony, without sacrificing their own way of life. Says Brown, "In England you see that the Jews stick to their culture, the Greeks the same, the Pakistanis, the French, the Dutch. Well I saw it was possible and wise to identify myself with being a Rasta."

Brown in front of the Rasta colours that make up the Ethiopian flag.

BURNING SPEAR

Born Winston Rodney, Burning Spear took his stage name from the spiritual name of Kenyan statesman Jomo Kenyatta. He is arguably the most uncompromising of all the Rastafarian reggae artists. From the very beginning of his career, Burning Spear distanced himself from what he saw as the frivolous, light-hearted, dance-based aspect of reggae music, preferring to leave that to other performers in the field.

SERIOUS STUFF

It is not surprising that Burning Spear's early recordings, which reflected his strong beliefs, were not commercially successful. They were more akin to traditional Rastafarian chanting than rude-boy posturing, and their improvised, jazz-based approach to recording made his singles inaccessible to many listeners. Still, no-one would deny the sheer quality of tunes such as 'Foggy Road', 'Swell Headed', 'Ethiopians Live It Out' and 'New Civilisation' and Spear did make the Jamaican Top 5 with 'Joe Frazier'.

MARCUS GARVEY

The overpowering influence for all Spear's writing came from the work of Marcus Garvey, the black civil rights leader; Garvey's own words feature prominently in the songs. Following his departure from the Coxsone Dodd organisation, Burning Spear and co-performers Rupert Wellington and

'Rocking Time'
June '74
'Marcus Garvey'
October '75
'Dry and Heavy'
May '77

'Social Living'
October '78
'Man In The Hills'
July '79
'Hail H.I.M.'
September '80

Delroy Hines recorded the spell-binding 'Marcus Garvey' in 1975 for producer Jack Ruby. The single, and album of the same name, brought fame and the album was released in the UK on Island. The word was that Burning Spear would shortly match Bob Marley's superstar status.

SOLITARY SPEAR

In fact, superstardom never came. Spear recorded one more album, 'Man In The Hills', with Jack Ruby, then took control himself, splitting from Hines and Wellington. 'Travelling', 'Free Black People', 'Spear Burning' and 'Throw Down Your Arms' highlighted his mesmerising vocal delivery and accomplished writing.

ENGLAND-BOUND

In 1976, Spear teamed up with Aswad. In '77, after a frantic day's rehearsal, they tore apart London's Rainbow Theatre: this compelling performance was captured forever by Island's mobile recording studio. In '78, Spear left Island and recorded 'Marcus' Children', (titled 'Social Living' in the UK). He had great respect for Aswad and took them back to Jamaica for the recording sessions.

ALBUM ARTIST

Burning Spear switched to EMI for his next classic, 'Hail H.I.M.'. Recorded at Marley's state-of-the-art Tuff Gong studio and produced by 'Family Man' Barrett, it confirmed Spear's reputation as an artist whose work seemed better suited to albums than singles. Never one for the catchy hook or cheap lyric, Spear writes songs that are reflective, spiritual and thought-provoking.

One of the most important reggae artists, he still tours the world in the late 1990s, delivering his soulful music to his many fans.

BLACK LEADER

Marcus Garvey is one of the most important figures in the history of black civil rights. He was born in St. Ann's Bay, Jamaica in 1887. Africans had been brought to Jamaica in the 1600s and 1700s by the British colonists, to work as slaves on white-owned plantations. Although slavery had been abolished by Garvey's time, blacks were treated as second-class citizens. Most black families, including Garvey's own, lived in poverty. Garvey urged fellow-blacks to assert themselves. He set up the Universal Negro Improvement Association and started the Back-to-Africa movement, encouraging black people to take pride in their African roots and look to Africa for an end to oppression. A gifted speaker and writer, he re-examined history – and the Bible – from a black perspective.

Garvey proclaimed: "We are the descendants of a suffering people. We are...determined to suffer no longer."

PRINCE BUSTER

Prince Buster came to ska and bluebeat music relatively late in life – his twenties. He had earned the name 'Prince' because of his ability to look after himself in boxing matches and street gang clashes. (The tough teen was also Coxsone Dodd's 'minder', protecting the legendary Downbeat sound system.) Buster Campbell's unusual first name was his father's tribute to the founder of the Jamaican Labour Party, William Alexander Bustamente.

A DEBUT CLASSIC

In 1960 Prince Buster gave up boxing in favour of music and made his first record, 'Oh Carolina' (the song that was to give Shaggy a chart-topping UK and US hit 35 years later). Buster had split from Coxsone Dodd, and set up his own business, The Voice Of The People, which ran record shops, sound systems and a record label. 'Oh Carolina' was a hugely impressive debut for the young Prince Buster, and he was soon collaborating with talented artists such as Arkland Park's Drumbago All Stars, the Les Dawson Blues Unit, the Rico Rodriguez Blues Band, the Folks Brothers and Count Ossie. Buster's first album, 'I Feel The Spirit', came out in '63, and only added to his growing reputation.

BUSTING OUT

'I Feel The Spirit'
May '63

'Fly Flying Ska'
July '64

'Fabulous Greatest Hits'
September '67

Prince Buster beat a lot of the competition by breaking into the international market. By the mid 1960s he was a cult figure in the UK. He was adored by the 'mods', and the large Jamaican community in London.

Prince Buster poses for the cover of his debut album, 'I Feel The Spirit'.

BLOCKBUSTER

Buster appeared on the popular 1960s TV music programme 'Ready, Steady, Go!' alongside such legends as the Rolling Stones, the Beatles and the Animals. He wrote about everything – Jamaican street violence, politics, his own childhood memories, and women. He had a huge influence on later reggae bands, including Madness (named after one of his songs), the Beat and UB40.

JUKE-BOX JURY

In the 1970s, Buster's income from his own recordings tailed off, but his canny investments in the outskirts of the music industry paid off. He monopolised the juke-box business in Jamaica. And his tough reputation helped him to retain an iron grip on his organisation.

THE PRODUCER

But Buster did not neglect his musical roots. He continued to perform and turned producer for many well-known Jamaican artists. Big Youth, Dennis Alcapone (whose name was also inspired by one of Buster's songs), John Holt, Dennis Brown, Alton Ellis, the Heptones and the Ethiopians all worked with Prince in the producer's seat. He soon realised that his classic back catalogue was his greatest asset, so he repackaged and re-released his earlier hits. Today, the Prince divides his time between his businesses and regular performances. He is enjoying new popularity. Following its use in a Levi's ad, his single 'Whine and Grind' hit the UK and US Top 10s in 1998.

ROVING RECORDS
Mobile sound systems such as Dodd's could make or break an artist and there was fierce rivalry between them. These trucks toured the island, booming tunes out of their big speakers, selling records and supplying 'stationary' record shops.

Sound systems were highly decorated.

Juke-boxes gave Buster a steady income in the '70s.

JIMMY CLIFF

Singer James Chambers' first venture into the recording business was not very encouraging, although his experience was not unique: "I made my first record for a tiny record company based in Kingston, Jamaica…'Daisy Got Me Crazy' was never released and I got no money for it. All they offered me was a shilling for my bus fare home which I refused. I thought it was an insult."

BUT THEN

Jimmy Cliff persevered. At the age of 14, he had a Jamaican No. 1 with 'Hurricane Hattie', recorded for Leslie Kong's label, Beverley. It was young Cliff who had persuaded Kong to go into the record business. He had written a song called 'Dearest Beverley' and he approached Leslie Kong to release it because he owned a Kingston restaurant called Beverley's.

NEW YORK, NEW YORK

Chris Blackwell, head of the Island record label, and long a champion of ska and reggae, spotted Cliff performing at New York's World Fair in 1964. Impressed, Blackwell whisked him back to England. But Cliff did not achieve overnight success – he toured pubs and clubs, often on backing vocals. In '65, ska was unknown in the UK. "They didn't really know what Jamaican music was. So in my nightclub act, I did two thirds rhythm and blues (R&B) and one third ska."

BEAUTIFUL BRAZIL

But success was just around the corner. Cliff submitted his song 'Waterfall', written in 1968, to a song festival in Brazil. Cliff went for a week – and stayed for a year!

Always touring, Cliff often supports major acts.

HOUSE OF EXILE
Many reggae artists are Rastafarians, but in 1972 Jimmy Cliff turned to Islam – as the black American activist Malcolm X had before him. From then on, Cliff became an outsider in his native Jamaica.

Cliff became a big star in Africa. He was one of the first artists to record there. "In Africa, I got the greatest satisfaction I've ever had as an artist. The acceptance and appreciation I received there, it made me feel so good. After all, the first song I'd ever written was 'Back To Africa'."

Perhaps Jimmy's proudest moment was when he played to 75,000 people – blacks *and* whites – in Soweto, South Africa.

'Hard Road To Travel'
February '67
'Jimmy Cliff'
December '69
'The Harder They Come'
January '72

'House Of Exile'
November '74
'The Best Of Jimmy Cliff'
March '76
'Give The People What They Want'
September '81

Inspired by Brazil and its people, Cliff wrote 'Wonderful World, Beautiful People', the song that brought him international fame. The single 'Vietnam' followed, which was extravagantly praised by Bob Dylan and Paul Simon.

SUPERSTARDOM!

In 1972, Cliff starred in 'The Harder They Come', a box-office smash about the reggae music industry. Neither the film nor its soundtrack made Cliff's fortune, but the movie was a cult 'classic', and is still screened today.

'The Harder They Come' brought reggae – and Jimmy Cliff – to new audiences around the world.

TROUPER

In the '70s Cliff made lengthy trips to Africa and Latin America, and the music and culture of these countries inspired and excited him. His music reflected these influences, and Cliff released dozens of singles during the '70s and '80s, though few were really successful. It would take 'Trapped', Cliff's song performed and recorded by Bruce Springsteen, and 'I Can See Clearly Now' to catapult Cliff back into the public eye. He continues to tour the world today, 36 years after refusing that shilling for his bus fare home.

DESMOND DEKKER

Could the glorious reggae which has poured out of Jamaica since the early 1960s have ever developed without the vision and talent of local producers? One of them, Leslie Kong, took on young Desmond Dacres (soon to be 'Dekker'). Orphan Dacres grew up in St. Thomas, but went to Kingston to work as a welder. He used to sing while he worked – so well that his colleagues encouraged him to turn professional.

ACE RECORDINGS

Singing with the Aces, Dekker's first single, 'Honour Your Father and Mother', was released in Jamaica and the UK in 1963. Dekker had no less than 20 No. 1 hits in Jamaica during the '60s, before making it in the UK charts with '007 (Shanty Town)' in '67.

THE PROMISED LAND?

Two years later, Dekker's 'Israelites' became the first reggae record to top the UK charts. It also entered the Top 10 in the USA – no mean feat as the USA was slow to appreciate Jamaican music. Desmond moved to England, where audiences lapped up his witty, observant songs. He came close to scoring another No. 1 with 'You Can Get It If You Really Want', written by Jimmy Cliff and featured in the film 'The Harder They Come'.

'Action!'
September '68
'This is Desmond Dekker'
May '69
'Israelites'
October '69
'Black and Dekker'
September '80
'King of Kings' (with The Specials)
October '93
'The Best Of Desmond Dekker'
December '93

KONG'S DEATH

In 1971, Dekker nearly gave up music when his long-time producer, Kong, died of a heart attack. He changed label but never repeated his early successes. In '84 he was declared bankrupt. He complained bitterly that he had never received the royalties he was due from his hits.

GREGORY ISAACS

Originally a panel-beater, Gregory Isaacs was quickly discovered by renowned producer Rupie Edwards. Singing with the Concordes, he made 'Another Heartbreak', 'Each Day' and 'Black And White'. Isaacs also worked for Prince Buster on 'Dancing Floor'. Dozens of other singles were released in the late 1960s and early '70s.

CONTROL FREAK

By 1973 Isaacs was established as a tough, uncompromising member of the reggae 'Mafia'. He set up the African Museum label in order to have more artistic control, though he still recorded for other labels in his search for success. In '74 his single, 'Love Is Overdue' (on Trojan) entered the UK charts.

'Extra Classic'
September '77
'Slum Dub'
April '78
'Soon Forward'
June '79

'Out Deh'
September '83
'The Cool Rider Rides Again –
22 Classic Cuts'
June '93

LIKE A VIRGIN

His reputation grew. In the UK Richard Branson, founder of Virgin Records, sat up and took notice. Virgin released Isaacs' 'Soon Forward' and 'Cool Ruler'.

BAD BOY

But then Isaacs' career suffered a setback. Personal and financial problems resulted in a jail sentence. His 'bad boy' image had caught up with him. On his release, he needed cash – fast. Isaacs recorded his new material with any label or producer who offered the right price. Luckily, his talent ensured that there was no artistic compromise and Isaacs, one of the great reggae artists, continues to produce reggae music of the very highest quality in the late 1990s.

Isaacs has worked for many producers in his long, distinguished career.

BOB MARLEY

Bob Marley was without doubt the most famous figure to emerge from the Jamaica-based reggae community. Sadly, on 11 May 1981, 36-year-old Robert Nesta Marley died from lung cancer and a brain tumour. The talented superstar left behind hundreds of classic recordings for reggae fans to enjoy.

IN THE BEGINNING...

Marley was born in 1945, the son of an English seaman and a Jamaican mother. At school he met Bunny Wailer and Peter Tosh who were to join him as pivotal figures in the Jamaican 'ska' movement. The trio went into the studio in 1965 to record the first of many singles as the Wailers. They enjoyed local success with 39 singles before finally producing their first album. Marley's music encompassed many styles during this period. He experimented with soul, rocksteady (romantic soul), ska and even close harmony 'doo-wop' styles.

UNIQUE PARTNERSHIPS

The I-Threes – Rita Marley, Marcia Griffiths and Judy Mowatt – provided a gospel sound.

In 1966 Marley married Rita Anderson, a talented singer working with local group the Soulettes. She would later become a member of his own group of backing singers, the I-Threes. Devout Rastafarians, Marley and his wife lived on a commune.

For the time being, the Wailers were all-male. Joined in '67 by brothers Aston and Carlton Barrett, the group began to work with the talented producer Lee Perry. In his spare time, Marley loved to play football and had his own team.

SUCCESS

In 1972 the owner of Island, Chris Blackwell, signed the band. Unconventionally, he gave them a large advance and trusted them to go back to Jamaica to record something for him. With their fixed line-up, the Wailers were the first reggae 'band' and their tremendous 'Catch A Fire' album of 1973 sold worldwide. The following year, UK guitarist Eric Clapton recorded Marley's witty but poignant song 'I Shot The Sheriff', which helped to raise Marley's profile even further. Tosh and Wailer left the band to pursue their own careers.

PEACEMAKER
Bob Marley was as passionate about his politics as he was about music. An attempt on his life in 1976 may have been due to his strongly held views. Marley, his wife Rita and his manager, Don Taylor, were all injured when gunmen burst into Marley's Kingston home and shot at them.

But political awareness brought about a proud moment in '78. Marley played the Jamaican One Love peace concert, where he persuaded Michael Manley, the Jamaican prime minister and Edward Seaga, the opposition leader to shake hands in front of the huge crowd.

Marley promotes political peace.

BLACK AND WHITE

Now backed by the I-Threes, Marley took his accomplished reggae music all over the world for the next five years and achieved superstardom. The gospel sound of the I-Threes was much more familiar to the rock-fed audiences of the day, and Bob Marley and the Wailers attracted new listeners to reggae. Reggae concerts no longer had an exclusively black audience – to the great delight of this peace-loving Rastafarian.

Just before his tragically early death, Marley headlined at a huge concert in the newly-liberated Zimbabwe. He was extremely proud to be associated with such a momentous event in the struggle for black liberation. In fact, his entire career played its own important part in this struggle.

Marley cut his first single, 'Judge Not' at the age of 16.

LEE PERRY

One of reggae's most adventurous – and longest serving – producers, Rainford Hugh Perry was born in 1939 in St. Mary's, Jamaica. He acquired a number of nicknames along the way: 'Little' Lee Perry would later be known as the 'Upsetter', 'Gong' and, most famously, 'Scratch'.

STARTING OUT

Perry started out in the music business at the bottom, selling records for the legendary Clement Coxsone Dodd from the boot of Dodd's car. Soon he was promoting and presenting Dodd's hugely successful Downbeat sound system. Coxsone recognised Perry's talents as a record producer and talent scout. Lee Perry would also become a prolific and popular recording artist in his own right.

His first record cunningly capitalised on a dance craze of the day called the Chicken Scratch: and a nickname was born! Perry soon fell out with Dodd. He wrote 'The Upsetter' – said to be a stinging attack upon Dodd – and another nickname stuck.

'The Upsetter'
June '69
'The Return of Django'
September '70
'Super Ape'
December '76

'Scratch on the Wire'
October '79
'The Upsetter Box Set'
September '85
'Arkology' (3 CD box set)
September '97

BUILDING THE ARK

In 1968 Perry took an important step. His reputation as a producer had been growing and he set up his own studio, the Black Ark, in his own back garden. Next came his own record label, Upsetter. He was astute. He encouraged and produced many unknown reggae artists. By '69, he had achieved success outside Jamaica. The Upsetters, a studio band assembled by Perry, had a Top 10 hit in the UK. However, his finest hour was to come. Lee Perry worked with Bob Marley and the Wailers and significantly contributed to their success. (Marley named his label Tuff Gong after Perry's newest nickname, 'Gong'.)

END OF THE ARK

Upsetter released over 100 reggae singles and dozens of albums during the period between 1969 and '74. But there were disturbing signs that all was not well. Perry had always been an eccentric, but something snapped. He burned down his studio and fled to Holland, a country known for its liberal attitude towards drugs. He soon relocated to London, where the punk scene was springing up, to work again with Bob Marley on 'Punky Reggae Party', released in '77.

After giving up Rastafarianism, Perry banned anyone with dreadlocks from his Black Ark studio!

THE MAD GENIUS

Although marijuana is illegal in Jamaica, many Rastafarians smoke it as a sacrament. Some say it brings about spiritual experiences.

It is impossible to tell to what degree Lee Perry's use of drugs contributed to what many people saw as a sad mental decline in the late 1970s. He suddenly denounced Rastafarianism and gave some puzzling interviews: "Good evening and greetings, you people of the universe. This is Lee 'Scratch' Perry, madder than the mad, greater than the great, rougher than the rough, tougher than the tough and badder than the baddest. We are here at the turntable terranova – it means we are taking over."

Madder than the mad? Possibly. Genius? Certainly.

Lee Perry: "We're taking over the star!"

RESPECTED PRODUCER

Despite his bizarre behaviour, Perry has a well-deserved reputation as one of the greatest producers of all time. The 1980s saw collaborations with talented UK dub producers the Mad Professor and Adrian Sherwood. Today, Lee 'Scratch' Perry is still recording, and has become a much-respected icon for the drum 'n' bass and jungle generation.

SLY and ROBBIE

It's unusual for session musicians to make a name for themselves, but that is precisely what Sly and Robbie did. Record producers often bring in session musicians when they have a clear idea of the sound they want to create, but neither the patience nor money to waste valuable studio time while band members practise on unfamiliar instruments.

Enter the session musician: someone who can take one look at a written part, then play it without a mistake. In fact, top-class session musicians throw the 'dots' (printed music) out of the window, and respond with their hearts rather than their heads. Sly and Robbie not only did that, but they created their own 'sound' in the process.

STAR SESSIONISTS

Sly Dunbar is a genius on the drums.

Drummer Lowell Charles Dunbar got the nickname 'Sly' because of his admiration for the American funk band Sly and the Family Stone. Dunbar was playing with Skin, Flesh and Bones when he met up with bass player Robbie Shakespeare in 1975. Their musical styles and approach to reggae gelled instantly. They made their name producing 'The Right Time' for the Mighty Diamonds and the word got around fast that Sly and Robbie were *the* rhythm section if you wanted to add gloss and panache to your recordings. Sly and Robbie have played on countless reggae records, working with the Upsetters,

'Disco Dub'
May '78
'Reggae Greats'
October '85
'Rhythm Killers'
September '87

'Silent Assassin'
June '90
'Reggae Hits 1987-90'
June '91

U-Roy, Bunny Wailer, Peter Tosh, Black Uhuru, Burning Spear and many others. They became known as the 'dynamic duo', or the 'rhythm twins'.

Sly and Robbie with Black Uhuru, for whom they produced the ground-breaking 'Showcase'.

CALL A TAXI
The pair formed their own record label, Taxi, and produced many hit singles for Jamaican artists. In the late '70s, Sly Dunbar recorded two 'solo' albums, 'Simple Sly Man' and 'Sly, Wicked and Suck', which featured – of course – Robbie Shakespeare on bass. Soon the pair were in great demand outside the close-knit reggae community. International pop superstars such as Joan Armatrading, Bob Dylan, Ian Drury and even John Lennon's widow Yoko Ono were queuing up for their services. They also provided the beats for Jamaican-born singer Grace Jones' best-selling dance album, 'Nightclubbing'.

Sly and Robbie's mechanical beats were called 'robotic' by some and they certainly anticipated the sounds of the digital age of drum machines and sequencers.

Shakespeare provides innovative bass sounds for many artists.

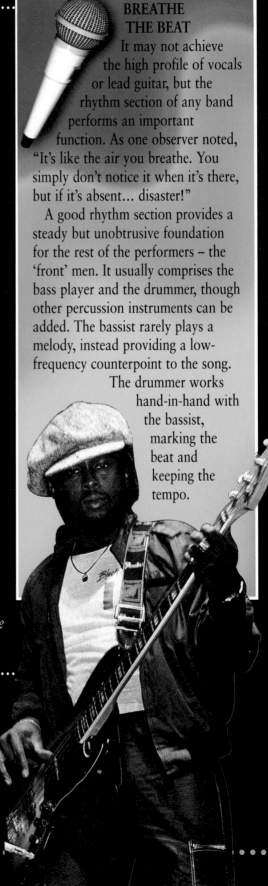

BREATHE THE BEAT
It may not achieve the high profile of vocals or lead guitar, but the rhythm section of any band performs an important function. As one observer noted, "It's like the air you breathe. You simply don't notice it when it's there, but if it's absent... disaster!"

A good rhythm section provides a steady but unobtrusive foundation for the rest of the performers – the 'front' men. It usually comprises the bass player and the drummer, though other percussion instruments can be added. The bassist rarely plays a melody, instead providing a low-frequency counterpoint to the song.

The drummer works hand-in-hand with the bassist, marking the beat and keeping the tempo.

INTO THE DIGITAL AGE
The new technologies did not deter Sly and Robbie. Their 'Murder She Wrote' and 'Tease Me' albums, produced for Chaka Demus and Pliers, were both UK hits. Sly experimented, mixing in the Asian pop sound of bhangra to take ragga to new heights.

After a career spanning three decades, the best rhythm section in Jamaica can still produce the goods!

TOOTS and the MAYTALS

Frederick 'Toots' Hibbert made history by releasing the first ever record to have reggae in its title – 'Do the Reggay'. In the early 1960s he had formed a 'ska' vocal trio along with Nathaniel 'Jerry' Mathias and Henry 'Raleigh' Gordon, for the influential disc jockey and recording company boss Coxsone Dodd. Toots had a very distinctive voice: strong, sometimes raucous, but very soulful. This voice launched him into a career that has so far lasted nearly 40 years.

EARLY DAYS

Hibbert was born in May Pen, Jamaica, but in the late 1950s he moved to the notoriously tough Trenchtown district in Kingston. Hibbert was working as a barber: "I used to sing all the time, and people would come around and listen, and say I was good and I should go and record my voice. That's when I met Raleigh and Jerry. They came around and said they liked my singing and wanted to form a group…"

The Maytals' first record, 'Hallelujah', was an instant success in Jamaica. More local hits followed, also on a religious theme, such as '6 & 7 Books of Moses', 'Shining Light' and 'He Will Provide'. Then they moved to Dodd's rival, Prince Buster. Toots and the Maytals enjoyed several more hits, but in 1966 they switched labels again, this time to Byron Lee's BMN company.

'The Sensational Maytals'
June '66
'Never Grow Old'
October '66
'Funky Kingston'
June '73

'Reggae Got Soul'
October '78
'Do the Reggae 1966–1970'
December '88
'Sensational Ska Explosion'
October '93

This rare debut album was later re-released as 'Sensational Ska Explosion'.

RECORDING SENSATION

The same year, they won the Jamaican Song Festival. These annual festivals showcased reggae bands. Like the sound systems, they played an important role in promoting reggae music.

After this success, the Maytals seemed never to be out of the Jamaican charts. 'Bam Bam' was followed by 'Fever', 'It's You', 'Never You Change' and 'Daddy'. The year also saw the release of their first album, 'The Sensational Maytals'.

TIME INSIDE

However a temporary halt to their growing success was just around the corner. Toots was jailed after being caught in possession of marijuana. On his release, Toots moved to Leslie Kong's Beverley label, and wryly enjoyed his biggest success to date with '54-46 That's My Number'. It referred to his prison number!

MENTO MENTOR

Mento was the first recorded Jamaican music and had a big impact on many reggae artists. It drew on a mixture of musical genres, notably the traditional work songs sung by the plantation slaves and the music of the Pocomania Church, where Toots Hibbert had been a chorister as a boy. As in the US Baptist Churches, this music featured lots of percussion, clapping and foot-stamping.

Mento also borrowed rhythms from the marching bands of carnival (Jonkanoo), and from the quadrille, a ballroom dance that had been popular with the European settlers.

Other influences came from nearby Cuba, for example rumba, bolero and mambo, while from black America came the big-band sounds of swing, and of course, rhythm and blues (R&B).

FAME AT LAST

Toots' records had been imported to the USA and the UK for many years for a small group of fans, but in 1976, Toots knew he had made it at last when he received this glowing review: "Toots Hibbert is unquestionably one of the greatest vocalists to appear in popular music in the past decade".

From then on, Toots and the Maytals could fill venues in major cities all over the world whenever they chose to jump

A traditional mento band performs on the streets of Kingston, Jamaica.

on a plane. In 1980, Toots achieved another historic first, when 'Toots Live', recorded in London's Hammersmith Palais, went on sale in the shops...just 24 hours after it was recorded!

REGGAE's influence

Reggae has had an enormous impact on the world of pop music. First came the 'ska' sound of the Specials and the Beat, then UB40's crossover pop. Artists such as Shaggy and Shabba Ranks explore dancehall ragga, while dub has spawned the likes of Dub Syndicate and US3. Today, jungle and drum 'n' bass tunes are popular in clubs across the world, to the extent that DJs such as Goldie can achieve star status.

UB40

Sons of a respected Scottish folk singer, Ali and Robin Campbell looked beyond their father for their musical influences – to the West Indies, 6,500 km away. The Campbell Brothers were joined by fellow reggae enthusiasts Earl Falconer, Mickey Virtue, Brian Travers, Jim Brown, Norman Hassan and Astro.

TRIBUTE TO THE KING

In January 1980 UB40 released 'King', a tribute to the assassinated black civil rights leader, Martin Luther King. The record went straight into the UK Top 10, and the band were on their way. They toured with top pop group the Pretenders during the same year, which helped to bring them to more fans. In August, their first album was released.

BAND WITH A MESSAGE

The early 1980s was a time of severe unemployment in the UK, especially among the young. Previously out of work themselves, the band named themselves after the unemployment benefit (UB) form number 40. They were fiercely critical that the government of the day was unsympathetic to the unemployed and used their debut album as well as their choice of name to highlight the problem. The album was entitled 'Signing Off'.

'Signing Off'
August '80
'Present Arms'
May '81
'Labour Of Love'
September '83

'UB40'
May '88
'The Best of UB40: Vol One'
October '87
'The Best of UB40: Vol Two'
October '95

This is the expression used when one gains full-time employment, and no longer needs to 'sign on' each week to receive benefit. Its cover featured a blow-up of the notorious form.

Chrissie Hynde (centre) made two hit singles with UB40.

LITTLE LABEL

UB40 formed their own label, DEP International and, still highlighting the plight of the unemployed, released the single 'One In Ten', which gave them their second Top 10 hit. The band didn't look back. Five singles later, 1983 brought them two No. 1s in the UK charts. The single 'Red, Red Wine', and their album 'Labour Of Love' sold worldwide.

FROM DOLE TO SUPERSTARDOM

UB40 began to tour the world and concentrated more on their love of 'rasta'. Although the A-sides of their singles were always accessible pop songs, the band stayed true to their first musical love. They craftily promoted reggae sounds to their pop audience by featuring a heavy dub version of each song on their B-sides.

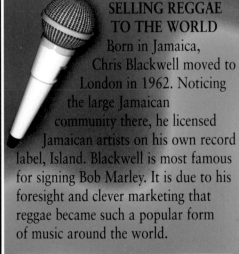

SELLING REGGAE TO THE WORLD

Born in Jamaica, Chris Blackwell moved to London in 1962. Noticing the large Jamaican community there, he licensed Jamaican artists on his own record label, Island. Blackwell is most famous for signing Bob Marley. It is due to his foresight and clever marketing that reggae became such a popular form of music around the world.

DRINKING IN SUCCESS

It was not surprising that UB40 wanted to take part in the 1988 Nelson Mandela concert with fellow reggae fans, Special AKA. They played 'Red, Red Wine'. It gave them their first US No. 1 and they have never looked back.

Chris Blackwell founded Island Records.

The SPECIALS

Perhaps one of the bands that owes most to Jamaican music is the Specials. Formed as Special AKA in 1979, the band featured a multi-racial line-up.

INSTANT SUCCESS

The band formed their own label, Two-Tone Records, to release 'Gangsters', their first single. It was an instant hit. 'Too Much, Too Young' gave the Specials their first No. 1. As always, the song reflected their reggae influences. In addition to their own songs, they covered material by the Skatalites, Bob Marley and many other Jamaicans. But just four more hits followed, including the atmospheric 'Ghost Town', before the band split.

'The Specials'
October '79
'More Specials'
September '80

'In The Studio'
June '84
'The Specials: Singles'
August '91

THE POWER OF MUSIC

Singer Jerry Dammers took the name Special AKA with him and became involved with Artists Against Apartheid. In 1988, to promote a concert in aid of their campaign to free the African National Council leader, Dammers re-released his hit 'Nelson Mandela', retitled 'Free Nelson Mandela (70th Birthday Remake)'. Perhaps in a small but important way Dammers helped to change history?

The Specials were Jerry Dammers, Terry Hall, Neville Staples, Lynval Golding, Roddy Radiation, Sir Horace Gentleman and John Bradbury.

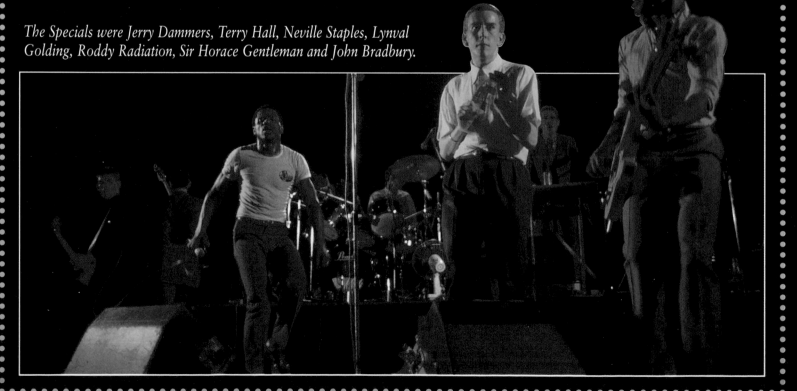

MADNESS

One of the most successful UK bands to embrace rasta music was Madness. Madness took their name from an early Prince Buster song and their first single, 'The Prince', was their tribute to his influence. It was released in 1979 on the newly-formed Two-Tone label.

PRINCE BUSTER'S CHILDREN

Madness didn't have to wait as long for success as their hero had. 'The Prince' entered the UK Top 20 and within months Madness recorded their first album. Staying faithful to their mentor, their second single, 'One Step Beyond' was a Prince Buster song – and it took them straight back into the charts.

Madness' entertaining, witty and astute ability to fuse their ska, bluebeat, reggae and rock influences paid off. The band enjoyed 24 Top 20 singles between 1979 and '86. Most of their songs were tongue-in-cheek observations of ordinary life in the '70s and '80s. Despite their popularity, in '86 Madness called it a day.

'One Step Beyond'
October '79
'Absolutely'
September '80

'Madness'
March '83
'Keep Moving'
February '84
'Madstock'
October '92

MORE MADNESS

However 1992 saw a brief reunion of the whole band. They played at a festival in London's Finsbury Park, and fuelled by media interest, three re-issues entered the charts during the same year: 'It Must Be Love', 'House Of Fun' and 'My Girl'.

The band were understandably pleased when 'One Step Beyond', a musical which highlighted the plight of London's homeless, opened in London in '93. The show featured 15 Madness songs. A tribute indeed to a band which had always tried to be a voice for the poor and disadvantaged.

GAZETTEER

The previous chapters have only been able to scratch the surface: dozens of other talented reggae musicians have been performing their inspiring music during the last four decades.

The Heptones

ISLAND SOUNDS

The Heptones, the Mighty Diamonds, Bunny Wailer, Peter Tosh and Big Youth are just some of the other classic reggae artists to achieve international success with their music.

The Skatalites were one of the most prolific and shortest lived reggae outfits, recording for producers Dodd, Prince Buster and Duke Reid. In the year they were together, 1964–'65, the Skatalites backed most of the talented singers of the day – including the Maytals, Jackie Opel and the Wailers – and produced some fantastic instrumental tracks in their own right, such as 'Tear Up', 'Beardman Ska' and 'Shot In the Dark'.

The Mighty Diamonds

Millie

REGGAE WOMEN

Although Black Uhuru was fronted by the talented Puma Jones, women in reggae are few and far between. The I-Threes probably achieved the most success. However, one female pop (not reggae) star deserves a mention. Millie was the first Jamaican to have a hit outside her native island, with the phenomenally successful pop song 'My Boy Lollipop', which sold seven million copies.

The Skatalites

CINEMA

Films such as 'The Harder They Come' played an important part in popularising reggae. The classic 'Rockers' was made in 1977 and starred Gregory Isaacs, Burning Spear and Robbie Shakespeare, among others.

Black Uhuru

Steel Pulse

US REGGAE

It was not until the 1980s that US reggae stars appeared, such as Bobby Kondors ('The Heads') and Shinehead ('Pepper Seed'). The '90s brought reggae superstardom to Shaggy ('Boombastic').

REGGAE'S SECOND HOME

Reggae has always been particularly appreciated in the UK. In the 1960s Clement Dodd and Duke Reid regularly brought over their awesome sound systems.

Many British bands, including Misty and Roots, the Clash and Steel Pulse, took their inspiration from Jamaica.

More recently Finlay Quaye recorded the excellent album 'Maverick A Strike'. Renowned for his Bob Marley covers, Quaye picked up a Brit Award for his reggae-inspired sound.

Bunny Wailer

FESTIVAL OF BRITAIN

Back in '74 fans in the UK were able to sample the genuine article. London's Wembley hosted a Caribbean Music Festival. It featured Bob and Marcia ('Young, Gifted and Black'), Desmond Dekker, the Maytals, the Pyramids, and Jackie Edwards (the singer who helped Chris Blackwell set up Island). Much of the film, 'Reggae' was shot there, "successfully capturing the infectious happiness of the music and the singers".

Finlay Quaye

Big Youth

INDEX

PHOTOGRAPHIC CREDITS *Abbreviations: t-top, m-middle, b-bottom, r-right, l-left, c-centre.*
Front cover & 14bl – Richie Aaron / Redferns. Cover bl, 22-23 & 31b – John Kirk / Redferns. Cover bm, 4-5, 8t & 9 – Fin Costello / Redferns. Cover br, 17bl & 25t – Simon Ritter / Redferns. 3, 14t & br, 16t, 17t & br, 20-21, 21m & 28t – Retna. 5t – Mike Cameron / Redferns. 6 & 31b – Mick Hutson / Redferns. 6-7, 7b, 10t, 18-19, 24t, 26-27, 27b & 28b – David Redfern / Redferns. 7m, 8b, 11b, 12 both, 13t, 19b, 21b, 23t, 24b, 25b, 30ml & b – Adrian Boot /Islandlife. 8-9 & 29b – D. Cronin / Redferns. 10b – Tim Hall / Redferns. 11t & 15mr – Ian Dickenson / Redferns. 12-13 – Michael Ochs Archive / Redferns. 13b & 31tr – Glen Baker / Redferns. 15ml, 18t & 27t – Ronald Grant Archive. 16m – Rogan Coles / Redferns. 18b – Graham Baker / Redferns. 19m, 22t – Island Records. 20 – Des Willie / Redferns. 22b, 23b, 26, 31tl & mr – Ebet Roberts / Redferns. 29t – Greg Mankowitz / Redferns. 30t – A. Putler / Redferns. 30mr – Rafael Macia / Redferns.